# Possessing Yourself

# Possessing Yourself

*Poems by Tim Kahl*

CustomWords

Published by CustomWords
P.O. Box 541106
Cincinnati, OH 45254-1106

ISBN: 9781934999585
LCCN: 2009928572

Poetry Editor: Kevin Walzer
Business Editor: Lori Jareo

Visit us on the web at www.custom-words.com

# Acknowledgments

| | |
|---|---|
| *Apalachee Review* | "The Unnatural Man" |
| *Berkeley Poetry Review* | "Headspin Sandwich" |
| *Brokenplate* | "Interpretation of Life in a Fishbowl" "The Undertaker's Sale" |
| *Carquinez Poetry Review* | "A Perfect Day of Kickball" "Baptism" |
| *The Chrysalis Reader* | "The Exit Tamer" |
| *Coffee & Chicory* | "Confidences" |
| *A Compass Rose* | "A Wisdom Fable" |
| *Eureka Literary Magazine* | "Mail File" |
| *Fox Cry Review* | "The Janitor of Souls" |
| *Hampden-Sydney Poetry Review* | "The Sense on the Streets" |
| *La Luna (Poetry Unplugged at Luna's Cafe Anthology)* | "Interpretation of Life in a Fishbowl" |
| *Midnight Mind* | "Look Under 'Minnows' in the Kinsey Report" |
| *Midwest Quarterly* | "The Naturalist" |
| *Minnesota Daily* | "American" |
| *Nightsun* | "Crusade" |
| *North Dakota Quarterly* | "The Call To Evening Prayer" |
| *ONTHEBUS* | "Possessing Yourself" |
| *Oregon East* | "Adequacy" "The Veterinarian" |
| *Poet Lore* | "Hominid Love Letter" |
| *Princeton Arts Review* | "Camp Empathy" |
| *Sacramento News & Review* | "Phallocrypt" |
| *Sanskrit* | "Mail Order Doll" |
| *Slipstream* | "Vitalis" |
| *Solo* | "Missing the Leonids" |
| *Spoon River Poetry Review* | "Loss of Rapture" |
| *Square Lake* | "Heliocracy" |
| *Wisconsin Review* | "Truisms" |

Thanks to the three Freds (GrossFritz, ZweiterFritz, DritterFritz), Margaret, Tracy, Terry, and Kristina, Soren and Reiner. Also, special thanks for courage, guidance and friendship along the way to S. Jhoanna Robledo, Ted Nourie, Joe Mattei, Lawrence R. Smith, John Engman, Joshua McKinney, Jeff Knorr, Danny Romero, Brad Buchanan, Scott Weiss, Rain Ananael, Jordan Reynolds, Maddy Walsh, Joe Atkins, Joshua Clover, Matthew Schmeer, David Koehn, Shawn Pittard, and Forrest Gander.

Thanks to Kevin Walzer and Lori Jareo and everyone at Word Tech Communications for believing in the manuscript.

# POSSESSING YOURSELF

*for all those who are genuine fakes*

# Table of Contents

## I.

## II.

# III.

# I.

Peer Gynt:   Have I not been-? I could almost laugh!
             Peer Gynt, then, has been something else, I suppose!
             No, Button-moulder, you judge in the dark.
             If you could only take a look at me at the end of my reins,
             you'd find only Peer there, and Peer all through,

                  — Henrik Ibsen


             tr. by R. Farquharson Sharp

## Possessing Yourself

Having nearly died in electro-shock, the later,
existentially speaking, I came to my own fiction
not really reproducible *en masse*, but as a scrapiron
heap of a man, yet wholly functional unit, certainly
as ambiguous as I now plainly stand here

with comments leaking in off of valuable documents
in your possession. Before there was a greater need
for me, a deep need shall we say, to underscore
my responsibilities which in childhood I had seen
as the way to meet the challenge of my empowerment

head on — from which often there is never a return.
To be honest one can never return or else one would
be left holding nothing or something more similar
to the way it had all started. And this is where we
get off thinking exactly as we are told to think. Though

each time we are told this the rules are drawn
a little differently. For others I have known,
the actual events are very simple. Myself, I constantly
deny the degree to which it can happen, if it happens
at all. I can't impress upon you heavily enough

the times I have regarded just this. The sheer possibility
of finding answers strikes me as the closest thing we have
to that pure thought which needs no further explanation
in the first place. That tree, or those tangelos,
if given a chance to speak, aren't likely to say anything

different either. But what illustrates this more aptly
is that, without recognizing it, the truth is always compliant
with every soul of every thing — a rockface, garden, sea horse
or north wind. The only consideration is how it is all arranged.
Today we can beg the question for this ordering principle

but previously I can tell you we had only to guess
at the proof. Which, in this case, is shaded a slight bit
off-center, but still really works if it is given
a chance. Go ahead. Try it. Turn it on here while
I gather my thoughts in this afternoon calm.

# All Cured

My beginnings were
given to me
by a man who worked
in the steel industry.
My mother went along
with him to Minnesota
on fishing trips.
Those were my family's
only vacations.
My brothers and
I still love the smell
of Norway pine; I love
the sound of loons.
But in the end we are
all cured
of our sentiments.

# The Naturalist

You are gone now and I am still the child.
I have nothing to give you for where you're going
except the few small creatures I have seen recently —
a crow hopping on its one good leg, the neighbor's
old cat hidden under a bush, still as a stopped clock.
Then I look closer, inspecting torn feathers and june bug
carcasses, snail tracks that dead end at a step up.
I find a mockingbird chick in the yard with
its mouth open, demanding more. But there will be
no more, nothing in the eyedropper can save it.
The chick fell from the nest, its eyes only slightly open,
still too innocent to be of much use to anybody, still too needy
to understand what has happened to it. And I won't even name
it, because names are for the living. Because you gave me
two names from the book that made you. Timothy. James.
But even the Bible can't explain why it is our nature to
endure despite what turns up missing. So I watch
the empty nest harden, continuously studying the remains
   . . . I am some species of naturalist, measuring loss
by paying close attention to all the buried vestiges.

# Overengineer

My father's idea of beauty is
a machine that is designed to hold up
under a load that no man would think
to put it under. I like to argue with
him that human flesh is more beautiful.
But we are both right because the body
lasts despite the weight of the cross
it carries for all of the world's people.

# Vitalis

The stand-up, cardboard Vitalis sign promised
a life that was someone else's, a life of
a slick-haired gentleman whose future was
in finance. The ads never pictured his hands.
They never showed anything below his pressed lapel
and starched collar. A Vitalis man was a man
for every woman who dared to put on a red dress.

My grandfather draped the white apron
around the butcher's apprentices and drugstore
clerks who came to get their hair cut.
They told their friends — the mechanics at
the Standard, the color TV salesmen,
the drivers of Geifman's delivery vans,
and the cooks at the Chuck Wagon —
all appeared in the pneumatic barber chair,
my grandfather dutifully circling around them,
attentive to the flat spots on each of their heads,
his sterilized scissors poised in the air.

I was ready for my crew cut in the horsey
chair where my grandfather hypnotized
my cousins and me with his electric razor.
The buzz of it on the back of my neck made me numb.
I was struck dumb by all the hair on the floor that
belonged to no one. I stared intently at all of it,
figuring out which pile looked like
it came off the skin of a dangerous animal.
For my safety, I was told never to walk
across the floor of the barber shop in
stocking feet because the hair would cut
like the sharp edges of shattered glass.
But nothing cuts so deep as the cold in
Davenport, Iowa and the memory of men with
their sides trimmed like eager recruits.

How could I know these men would be marching off
to face the ambush of winter? My grandfather joined
them, shoveling snow onto the embankments over his
head, scraping the ice off the windshield of his
sedan, prying off the frozen lid of the trash tins
in the alley, his hands so chapped they could

only be healed by the old world remedy of urine
rubbed onto them. What did I know as a boy of
the reasons palsy eventually sets in,
of why Murray from the dance studio across
the street stopped coming as frequently
for his afternoon trim? My world radiated out
and ended ten feet in front of me. It starred me,
dragging my hand over the stubble of my head,
playing tiddly winks for penny stakes on
the kitchen table, tugging on the string of
a pull-toy that made a girl's arms and legs
fly up in the air. I turned smooth stones in the dark
of my pocket. I put on my grandfather's gloves
to see if I could fit where his hands had been.

# A Perfect Day of Kickball

What made me leave Scott Montgomery's birthday party that day
was Susan Hanaway's braids. She had braids like my
grandmother did in the morning before she draped them
into an arch on the top of her head. So many times I had studied how
my grandmother's long hair changed into the country-girl style of a
Schleswig-Holstein mädchen. I had to leave the party because I wanted
to peek and see if Susan looked the same.
    Susan wasn't afraid of the kickball.
She could run at full speed and catch it. She wore an undershirt, not
a training bra. She got picked early and usually led off in the batting
order when she played kickball with the boys during recess. So, it was no
surprise that she came out to play kickball that day.
        We used trees as bases,
and a burned-up patch of grass served as the plate.
The ball was underinflated so we couldn't kick it very far, just
far enough to keep each other running inning after inning.
After a while we forgot to keep score, just Susan Hanaway and me
pitting our wills against each other like two little gas spills spreading in
overlapping circles, waiting for a match. We were lost in the euphoria of
pure sport, which only sport can provide for two kids who are dreaming
of growing up and knowing each other when they get older.
        Scott came over to tell me it was time for me to go home.
    I was always forgetting to go home.
            Two years later my home moved away from
that suburb of Chicago, and I never saw Susan again.
There have been no tomboys since her. Now my grandmother has
passed on, and nobody remembers how much time she spent in front
of the sink doing her hair. I am in my sixth city since Chicago, and
sometimes I think I see her braided arch of hair at the market under
the freeway where the old *babushkas* scurry around putting potatoes in
their burlap sacks. I see whole families crowding around tables full of
produce. The mothers are herding their kids into a more manageable
pack, flashing familiar smiles at their husbands. They look comfortable,
like they've been living in this town since they were little girls.
        I watch a girl in a feed cap unload bags of oranges from a
pickup. Her overalls make her look square and very serious, like the
body that is underneath does not belong to this age of spandex in
commercials. The girl is wearing braids all the way down her back, and
suddenly I am lovestruck as she tosses a bag of grapefruit she has sold
me, thinking I'll be able to catch it, thinking I'll be able to hold my own
with her this instant. But the bag falls and tears. The grapefruit scatter
and roll, and as I hurry to retrieve them, the girl shows me a smile

I recognize as being from the old country
— as perfect as any day of kickball I can remember
when no one could remember what inning or the score.

# The Veterinarian

How many more mornings will greet me with an alarm?
Today is one of those mornings set to go off at
first light when I wake and forget, the same as anyone,
what the day ahead would have me do. For a second,
my purpose escapes me — am I the grass planted to
spread across the side of the hill, or the wintering
bear dreaming of a cloudy day in April? Or should
I simply call my brother who has just planted a flag to
claim another year in his forties? He tells me
the story of two ducks flying side-by-side;
suddenly one runs into a transmission wire and
falls to the ground like a dropped scoop of chocolate.
The bird is barely alive. My brother brings it home
to nurse it back to health like the robin in
the cardboard box when he was twelve. But the
robin died too. Wild birds don't appreciate
the life-sustaining force that flows through
a garage. However, my brother tells me, if a bird
dies in your garage, it shouldn't go to waste.
So he hangs it by the swing set to let it bleed,
and that night he goes to bed thinking things
turned out best that he didn't become a veterinarian.
He dreams of being an expert carver of
road kill. He dreams of fish heads talking back
from the slop bucket. Then in the morning,
the alarm goes off, and as he rises, he hesitates.
He puts himself together. Forty-some-odd years
have brought him to this urgent day ahead,
and when he realizes he must go outside
to check the duck, he finds that during the night
the neighborhood cats have managed
to tear down the helpless carcass.

# Truisms

Would my brother still have learned the truisms
that every pickup truck driver knows, if John Wayne
hadn't changed his name from Marion Morrison?
Perhaps he would have taken after his trumpet teacher,
Mr. Galeardo, instead, whom my brother accused of tapping out
rhythms a little too close to his thigh. Now he sees gays
everywhere, sees the downfall of the country in them.
Nobody appreciates his sense of humor when he makes
these mock declarations. Making yourself look bad and thinking
it's funny is an inherited trait among all of my brothers. We see
self-deprecation as the path to a humbler version of nirvana.

Maybe my brother would have been a centerfielder like
Curt Flood. He would have had clear tasks to follow. He'd have been
happy just to throw a guy out at third or beat out an infield single. He
would have been the guy in the clubhouse who told jokes about himself
as a lefthander. And when he retired, he'd be the third base coach for a
contender in the minors, giving signals by shifting his groin
and rubbing his belly. And surely he'd wear
his personal misgivings as a badge of honor.
He'd grow bald, get slower, eat lard straight out of
the bucket, and make it all seem funny.

But when I last saw him, I said *Hey there, pilgrim, you're gettin*
*a little rounder in the middle. Can ya' still fit yourself behind the wheel*
*of your pickup?* He threw me down, stepped on me. It was
an accident he assured me. I didn't bother continuing to wrestle
with him. Resistance had been useless since childhood
when he practiced his wrestling moves on me — half-nelsons
in the bedroom, the chicken wing after dinner, and the dreaded
eichelberger which I think was just a name for some move he made up
that would inflict the most horrible punishment he could imagine. I was
screaming, hoping a person couldn't die from third-degree rug burns,
and he toyed with me the way a cat toys with its live dinner.
He stuck my face in his armpit and squeezed while he
imagined himself as the next Dan Gable.

They never had to take me off on a stretcher though.
I showered and I recovered. But sometimes I didn't shower
and my brother didn't shower either. Our sweat got mixed up
together on our skin and we let it sit there, drying, caked on for hours,
sometimes days. And one summer we ate a lot of fresh

onions from the garden and let the gods decide who could go longer
without a shower. Two weeks went by before they declared
a winner. And after, when we tried to burn our clothes, they wouldn't
catch fire. You know what they say: Blood is thicker than water.
To that one could add — sweat is thicker than lighter fluid.

Now when my brother is out on the road in his pickup driving
across his sales region, he judges men according to how much
cowboy they have in them. He sizes up their swagger, their
capacity for dignity, and their talent for cute expressions. If he
meets a man who needs tutoring, he never hesitates to share his
wisdom because that's exactly what The Duke would do. My brother is
not a centerfielder. He is not a wrestler. He is not a dreamer.
He is the man who taught his son to never look guilty.

And twice a week, as sure as a greenhorn's saddle sore,
I arrive at various houses in my neighborhood. I am a tutor for
students who are having problems in algebra and geometry.
They miss the details. They lack confidence. They seem unable to re-
member what the steps are, so I drill them over and over.
I drum the procedure into them — one, two, three . . .
one, two, three. My hands hold the cup of tea I've been given.
I sip and show them how to work through the hard problems
where all the answers are definite and true like the purpose of
a man in a white hat. I test them to see if they have
the basics down, if they can imitate the obvious,
if after a mistake or two, they can squint at the horizon
and see themselves as humbled heroes.

# Look Under "Minnows" in the Kinsey Report

In Chicago, where my eldest brother lives,
the skyscrapers inspire the awe of single men.
The lake inspires couples — its horizon is so stable.
Unwed women dream of the highway system. It can
take them anywhere with a cushion between
every car. In the fast lane of the Tri-State,
my eldest brother speeds up to catch the car
in front of him. It pulls over into the next lane.
My brother eyes the woman who is driving
and her small daughter. Then, he asks me,
*Why do little girls carry minnows in their pockets?*
It must be a crude riddle; he is apt to pose crude riddles
at this time in his life. The seamstress has left him.
The secretary moved back to her hometown.
The schoolteacher figured out they were wrong
for each other and now my brother is touching
people in the family a lot more than he used to,
but only their joints and muscles. His son looks on and
shakes his head. It is his first year in high school.
He is learning most of what he needs to know
in life from the locker room. The Kinsey Report
is still a few years away. Further still is a loved one's
constructive criticism. Then years of celibacy geared
to reforming the notion his best friend is his erection.

My brother slows down for the toll booth. He
tosses coins in the bucket, tries to leave before the light
turns green. He is being very patient waiting for my
answer to his riddle. I am thinking of Tammy Harness
who discovered those rotten bullheads in the bait box
on honeymooner's island with me. But Tammy only
carried a crawdad in her pocket. Her father had ripped
off its claws and Tammy kept it in her pocket for
three days until it was time for her to go back to Ohio.
I let her kiss me so I could see it. Maybe Tammy kept
the crawdad in her pocket because she wanted to be
like her older brother, the serious fisherman;
maybe it was bait for boys.

Only the silence of the highways can tease out the answer to
the riddle now. Later on the skyline of Chicago will
explain it to me, will fill up the junkyards and
vacant lots in me like the smell of a woman,

which has become a mystery again for my brother.
To understand this mystery better, he has consulted
*World Book*, the Kinsey Report, his
CD-ROM of the complete human anatomy,
but at this moment he has returned to the locker room,
turned to the crude riddles told there for guidance.
And, finally, I guess at the answer to his riddle. I am wrong.
I don't know my way around Chicago anymore either.
All the skyscrapers seem strewn like wreckage to me.

## Stark County

The beasts that trod upon the earthen path at
the county fairgrounds were cared for by
boys like me, but I knew nothing of cattle
except that they made excellent trail bologna.
The boys in the furniture store at Sugarcreek
ran the warehouse at my age.
They delivered a leather chair to
our door, up the interstate past the
belching blast furnaces of the Timken plant.
My mother made them coffee
while I listened to Cheap Trick in the basement.
The band played live at Budokan,
a place incomprehensible to me
for its large population of screaming girls.
The girls I met were steady, only interested
in boys whose jobs paid for ice cream
at the Milk and Honey. Eventually, they got
married to them and stayed in Stark County
to watch the demolition derby every year.
All of the amateur drivers plowed
into each other, understanding
that the one to suffer the least damage
would be the winner. The metal carcasses were
hauled off to a salvage yard in Massillon,
where boys like me tore out the seats and put them
in a Ranchero. We drove that beast once to
Uniontown for the Amish Scarecrow Festival.
The straw men were dressed up like us tourists.
We admired the likeness. The Amish boys
our age were working in the family restaurants,
clearing tables, washing dishes and carving chickens.
They directed traffic in the overcrowded
parking lot and eyed the Ranchero as we fled
with the radio on, picking up a signal from a station
in Cleveland that called itself the home of
the buzzard. We drove home leisurely,
poised somewhere between daydreaming and sleep,
longing to be home, still years away from
drinking coffee and years away from acting
the age of the responsible and the sullen.

# Camp Empathy

We named the dream of animals in hives and I was not
the man I had become when I returned from Camp
Empathy. The days and nights set against the reading
of newspapers and foreign periodicals. I developed
a rash certain I was enclosed in my very own suffering.

I remembered détente, Idi Amin, the blood of both
Kennedys, which smelled like newsprint. I brought my
wonder with me on our walks together. The early
afternoon sun pierced the forest canopy and left
patches of light on the ground that looked like
foreign countries. Each of us measured the shadows
we stepped into. The sun at dusk changed the shape of
the light patches. The edges became blurry. At night we
built a fire and continued with our reading.

We called the press the enforcer class. We had our
disagreements. We found every outlook to be another
helpless context. We were not there. This was the limit
of our experience. We discovered the networks had
never learned humility, but we could not act until the
images were released.

We were hidden away somewhere in America called
Camp Empathy. And in choosing sides there were
those who believed a televised Auschwitz could not
have happened and those who thought one learns to
live with spectacles the way one learns to live with
wrinkles. No one's cage is clean in
the post-simian amphitheatre.

We named the dream of animals in hives *The Glass and
Wire Apiary*. Each day began with the tiniest of voices.
They grew larger, but we were still learning by rote. On
the walks we took together, the sun lit up the paths we
were to follow. We got lost for different reasons.
We were from different generations. The longest days
were meant for travel, and, eventually we found Camp
Empathy again, before night fell. We followed a trail of
shiny objects on the leafy ground, things we were
certain we could faithfully set type with.

# The Exit Tamer

*for Frank Dillon*

He's the guy who taught me how to
drive in high school, made me do it right,
He taught me about speed,
eighty-five on the back roads to
Canal Fulton. The bumps made us fly.
I'd take the Pontiac out and practice speeding
until I told myself that I believed in it.
But my appetite was short-lived,
and now car sickness is always
looming, a vague threat
like sudden imprisonment for
past wrongs I've done to friends.

He drove me to high school every day,
showed up in a dozen different cars before
we reached graduation. He was always dealing.
There were trips to used car lots
and police auctions with him,
trips to parts stores in Massillon, trips to
softball practice and the fish fry afterwards,
trips to miniature golf where everyone
cheated on their score. There was no way of
knowing who might face punishment
for such meaningless deception.
There was no way of knowing that
by the time I had my degree, he'd be
matriculated into the void's dark institute.

I saw him last at his parents' house.
He was in the final months of regressive Hodgkins.
He joked that he was eating enough rice cakes and
yogurt for him to live to be a hundred,
yet we both knew that was unlikely to happen.
When I left, I told him to take care of his collie.
It was an awkward departure. He wanted me
to look him in the eyes and put my trust in him
again. He needed me to believe what
he had learned about resignation.
He knew that exiting was a lot like taming lions
— one forces a ridiculous invincibility.

So many of the people I've known
have quietly resigned themselves to something.
They knuckled under to consequences
and held on. It is a survival strategy.
Otherwise there is crippling disappointment.
This is what separates the young from the old.
The old resign themselves to comfortable postures.
The young drive all night to reach Cleveland;
there they head south to arrive by morning
in Canton, where a collie stands in the yard alone
barking at the kids in the neighborhood
loading themselves onto the bus.

At the funeral I said my goodbyes to friends,
and that was the last time I left Ohio. I'm not that good
at leaving. There is always one more clever
remark to add. And when my last bit of errant wit
fell into useless silence, I had the whole trip
back to Michigan to reprimand myself,
to revisit the days of all of us playing euchre in
the kitchen, to retrace the paths some lives take.
I steered for Toledo. The hum of the tires on the Turnpike
could have been his voice. His voice was a car horn
passing in the fast lane, confirming that it was
right there. I'm sure it was him. He was the guy
who always told me *we have to get off this exit here.*

# Olentangy

The stars were hidden from the city of Columbus and
there were shopping carts in the alley where the homeless
who lived off of discarded beer cans had left them. It was summer, the
year we shot bottle rockets at the Catholic Church
on the Fourth of July, the year we gave quarters to the locals
who sang folk songs on High Street. I was walking through
the alley to the house on Indianola Avenue where there was
enough rock n' roll and *Old Style* to let the night pass between us.
We were a bunch of guys in college ready to aim ourselves
at something larger than the Ohio we lived in, something
even larger than what we, as foul-mouthed critics, saw on
the television. But we met women anyway, told them
our vulnerabilities though they had been aware of them already.
We got lousy grades, made inept plans, but still championed
our virtues. This was before the time when there were "losers,"
so we were probably either genuine fools or foolish geniuses.
Eventually, we moved away from the house on Indianola Avenue, one
after the other, some back to hometowns in mid-Ohio, some to the
West Coast, some just headed back to Cincinnati.

We would meet on New Year's Eve in Covington a few
years later. Drunk on *Old Milwaukee,* I danced with
an enormous woman, put my head on her shoulder
and kissed her face fumblingly. She moaned and pressed
her breasts against me. She stared out at the bridge across
the Ohio River as though it were a star to wish on.
The "creekers" in me, on my breath, spoke to her.
I mumbled some affections, squeezed the flesh on her back
underneath her t-shirt and kept moving slowly to
the rhythm of the music. After midnight she disappeared,
I headed back to the hotel room with the guys to have
a few more beers, watch some TV, take my place beside
the keg and listen to Led Zeppelin. There would be no more
illusions that night, except the ones we would dispel while
drinking "creekers." The grand schemes we gave up on:
the self as explorer, colorblindness in America, the coming
of a new jazz age. We lost our innocence the instant we
stopped believing that we liked ourselves and started to
detail our failings.

Sometimes we got together for Super Bowls, once to hear
a friend of ours in Dayton play bouzouki. He was great, lightning fast

fingers — he was born to solo. He played covers and originals. He sang ballads from the old country, but he didn't seem too delighted about his situation in Dayton — working for his dad, still. He drank too much and we had to stop so he could puke by the side of the highway. Already the romance of the moment was diminished. Vomit on the breath tempers the notion of being "crazy-as-I-wanna-be." The head aching like a gut punch could have left any one of us standing out on a street in our hometown, drugged out and buckeyed, swearing to a billboard that there had to be some way to get out, some way we could find that feeling of invincibility we had as college students in Columbus, some way we could find that "Olentangy River of the mind."

We jogged to the 24-hr. Big Bear supermarket for some late-night breakfast. We ran home from the Thirsty I bar, yelling at cops like they were our sworn enemies. We shuffled back from Ohio Stadium in a crowd after our team had won big, exhilarated, passing around the bota bag filled with sweet drinks that etched our teeth. We did the High Street crawl, leaving tracks of booze and sweat like snails; then we got up and scrambled over the pavement, jumped off fire hydrants, each yelling *I'm Popeye, I'm Apollo's slut, and I sure do love da' guv'nuh.*

The nights were one long syncopated non sequitur. And in the morning our sweat tops and sweat pants leeched the toxins out of our body as we ran down along the banks of the Olentangy and discovered fresh muskrat prints in the black mud. We took notice of the flotsam in the gray stream of water drifting towards some non-descript end and we contemplated . . .

we contemplated the gospel according to philosophy 101, we contemplated the campus buildings we had been walking in and out of, we contemplated the whole unsuspecting sky above us, run through by the treetops. We were martyrs for the cause of recklessness, god damned independents who had come to crash the fraternities' parties. And, for years after, I wanted to live in a house like one of those great, brick fraternity houses, like one of those rambling, three-story, turn-of-the-century homes — perfect places to set up kegs and spout off the interminable amount of magic language we were learning which we thought would deliver us.

But a young man is measured by his prospects. He must be aware. He is set in the middle of the path of older men who have come before him and spread the future out across countries, continents, the globe, the galaxy, wherever their best and worst intentions have dared to follow them. And that is where Ohio is — the land of presidents:

31

Grant, McKinley, Harding, Hayes, Garfield, Taft, and Benjamin Harrison.

And it is the land of pornographers like Larry Flynt and Reuben Sturman. It is always a flower, a bird, a tree which has reminded us from those days that we were not chosen to represent Ohio. We were meant to let its myths work through us so we could be men standing on public property with our sons on our shoulders, pointing at what was to come down the river.

We will point and then take refuge in our lost innocence which still haunts us back from the time when we thought ourselves invincible, cradle to grave without ever becoming a homeowner. But now fear has found us, found us dreading the trips out to the mailbox to rip open some more envelopes. We fear we may come up lacking. We are afraid of losing, losing everything, now that our innocence has slipped us. It is fear that keeps the machinery moving forward, that slowly digests us. We are afraid that we were always meant to float downstream and get caught up in responsibility. We are afraid to drown and afraid to shake free, afraid to "lose it" in that one day we might wake up, take a crap out in the middle of the yard and yell at the dog to clean up afterwards. It is this fear that is humiliating us, but it is necessary.

This is what those nights on Indianola Avenue were telling us. They were telling us we were ordinary, we who let gravity force us to drink *Genesee Cream Ale* too quickly. The stars were hidden for a reason. We were not ready to accept them as decent neighbors, both slightly flawed and somewhat profane. We were testing them as symbols and our selves were wired up too, blinking on and off as the nights wore on, steering us toward professions that could not be imagined as of then. We came to know the sky in a trifling age. We are blameless then for what we did not recognize as important and what we have failed to get done. We must pass, anyway, in the direction of our prospects, we who have gotten on with it, we who wonder, we who are sick of improving our lives, we who have only just begun to learn how to despise ourselves for this.

# II.

"Does it hurt very much, *mashke?*" the girl asked Iktomi.

"Oh my, yes, but I am strong and brave," answered Iktomi, " I can bear it."

"I can bear it too," said the girl.

"It really isn't altogether unpleasant," said the girl after they did it a fourth time, " but I must tell you I don't believe you will ever get rid of this strange thing."

"I have my doubts too," answered Iktomi.

"Well, said the *winchincala*, one could get used to it."

"Yes, *mashke*," answered Iktomi, one must make the best of it, but let's try once more to be sure.

Brulé Sioux trickster myth

recorded by Richard Erdoes

# Migration

I go for a walk and pick up feathers. I think they are goose feathers. Many Canadian geese flock to this pond on my walking route before they head south. Several feathers are caught in a small whirlwind. They appear to me as dandelion carcasses caught in a March wind during spring in Ohio. Ohio was windy, windier than most imagine. The cemeteries in Canton were covered with dandelions, and the grackles flourished, their wings tested by flight from the nest, their nests built in silence. The geese are quieter today, perhaps expecting a change in the weather. They gather in the middle of the pond, and I try to guess the water temperature. Swimming in the water, their goose flesh and feathers are very stubborn to the cold. And the weather will get colder here, and they will keep coming. Russian Orthodox immigrants with their long beards come to pray here and baptize their followers at this pond in the middle of a city park in the middle of Denver. The pond will be dredged in the spring, and the bird crap of all the passing ducks and geese that has collected on the bottom will make something, somewhere else, a little greener.

# The Three Souls

All along the parkway the soul hides
in the bushes. None of its three parts
are damned. The *character soul* makes
a person recognizable; the *death soul*
lives on in the names and deeds
of the living; and *trickster soul*
insists the sound of snoring
is the sound of wailing women.

I have seen them together on the levee mid-summer —
*character* in the shade; *death* hanging from
a tree; the *trickster* knee-deep in the river
that tickles the city sleeping off its sickness.
They set traps there to catch us who wander
while whistling a made-up tune, who need
nothing but open sky to dream about, who recite
soliloquys to the infinitude of lingering questions.
Nobody watching. Just the three souls leer,
hungry for the recipes we have invented
— so many ingredients to litter our interior walls.
The decorations, cast-off, floating,
ornamental gourds drifting along the banks
while upstream the Yolo Bypass opens.

Mud eviscerated, the river exists on its staple diet
of fallen acorns. The outcroppings are abandoned altars
where the sweet fennel bathes its senses. A man
on a walk near the grove of oaks is drawn to the smell
of licorice. The three parts of the soul wait,
hidden, expecting to torture his imagination.

Then the ambush begins. A breeze like the breath
of an intent animal blows up from the Delta.
The soul captures its victim, a victim that pulls
like taffy, the three parts of the soul in a mènagé trois.
The victim's heart pumps, humming like an old
wall clock, but the *trickster* insists the hum is
a slim vibrator.

All three parts are busy. They reveal themselves
steadily in scenes of a funeral for a gray-eyed
clergyman; of an office closed for Easter (its lights
left on for the lilies); of a train heading south

to Bakersfield on the San Joaquin line. The souls
are alive in the carpet threads clinging to
the sleeves of illicit lovers who have spent
years admiring each other from afar,
who have let the sticks supporting them
bend with the weight of their libidos
— one a jazz lover, the other a gun owner.

And finally the river carries the damned away
to settle in the pools collecting on the hardpan.
Dimples of wildflowers stand erecting
their color into one more day. The three souls
flourish despite the changing conditions.
The *character soul* suddenly makes a man
visible. The *death soul* gives a man a name
and history, and the *trickster soul* is a realist
who has not yet decided what reality should be.

# Obedience School

Oh to be a dog in obedience school again —
when I learned to take commands from
a man with short hair and a whistle.
Every afternoon that summer I let my
wiry frame be guided by the spirit of
instruction, leaping in the air to catch
a frisbee and chasing after cheap little
props only to be tripped up by my own
bad habits in the end. I made my own kinds
of mistakes; then I'd have to sit and wait
and wait, left to brood upon my miscues until
I was released into a freshly mowed field
where I was free to languish in the multitude
of hollow praises I'd been given.

Those days of order, of single-minded
purpose — I learned all the skills I've
needed to survive. The goals I had were
clear; demands placed on me lacked any
hidden agenda. I was always ready to
perform. I stood on two legs and navigated
between the obstacles laid out in front of me,
every step thinking I'd been chosen as
an example for all the others who were
being tested. I learned trick after trick,
some of them invented just for me to learn.

I learned balance. I learned to roll over at
just the right moment. My days on earth were
measured by the tasks that I had mastered.
I had control; my choices were obvious.
But now I move between distractions.
My spirit flags because I lack precision.
I'm going through the motions, longing to
hear the sharp crack of the whip near my
ear so I can regain my edge, so I can see my
powerful hands out in front of me, grabbing
onto my training gear and never letting go.
I can almost hear the orders being given,
being drilled into me over and over and over
until I finally understand that I am human.

# The Unnatural Man

The unnatural man standing
on the banks of the Sacramento River
was rescued from a previous life
as a Halloween yard decoration.
I fished him out of the dumpster
and dug him into the shore
where everyone thought of him as
a monument to crossdressers.

When the water rose in the spring
it washed the paint off of him
up to his navel. The unnatural man
was dressed half in bodice,
half tuxedo, and the crows
landed on his shoulder and
mocked him for his bottom-half
made of knotty pine. It was clear
the unnatural man was just
a piece of lumber, but how he
stood out, covered with glitter,
on the banks of the restless river
where the solid earth and
the wind blowing through
the tules had given him a home —
the unnatural man in nature.

On the Fourth of July
I thought he might throw himself
into the river to escape from
all the insects. So I went down
to the river at night, the smell of
sulphur in the air, and
the unnatural man was missing.
During the long, dry summer
the stars had been bright, burning
evenly. Then, I thought I saw
one fall out of the sky, a shooting
star, or maybe it was a Roman candle.
If I could only tell the difference . . .
still I knew the unnatural man was
gone, a victim of inevitable selection.

# Mail Order Doll

From a catalog I received in the mail,
I ordered a doll that looked exactly like me.
I admit I was feeling a little bit lonely
with everyone off making adjustments
in their lives, learning new paths to
comfort, discovering fresh words
to describe what was gratifying.
I felt like an unpaired sock in a drawer
though I continued my rehearsals as
the center of attention; then when the doll
arrived, I didn't recognize it at all.
Sure, the shape of the face was the same.
It had the same placid gaze,
like it was staring out onto
a restless sea shimmering with
its own little private waves of joy.
Like me, it even sat in the lotus position,
had an ankle scar and arm freckles.
It could touch its toes and smile.
But I did not fall for its clever habit of
mimicking my unburdened sleep,
and I did not let it use my name
without first acknowledging to myself
that we had such different histories.
It was stuffed with polyurethane foam
and plastic beads, and I am full of longing
to be the kind of person who is
never discontented. Perhaps I could run
a simulation where my doll would
walk into a room full of people and
instantly like everyone in it.
I could provide all kinds of scenarios for it:
In each scene I could make it do
something outlandish. I could dream
what its hands might touch.
I might tempt the other doll masters
to come and play with me
just like we were in kindergarten.
And as soon as one of them says
I'm not playing right, I could take my doll
and go home to soak its head in
cold brine until it changed its ways.

I could discipline and punish it,
pick at its felt skin so that its innards
showed through. And there I would stand,
aged and decrepit, satisfied that I had held
together for so long despite the nagging feeling
of being emptied and the need to atone
for what has been delivered to my door.

# American

By the twilight's last gleaming
I saw your earth-colored Sioux eye
rise into high bluffs and spirit-song,
your body dressed like an American man
in drag, like Crazy Horse, who never
smiled for the camera. He was actual size.
His buried bones outran time zones
and media coverage and vending machines
while I'm here behind the wheel fighting
off a million addictions. I am grafted
onto tremors and fevers that launch
new product lines into the hidden
working model of my life.

I am a temperature of 102 on the Plains at noon
where country stations turn up like hitchhikers.
They both play the song of long black hair
and fill the passenger seat. Crazy Horse rides
shotgun with Coca-Cola. An infantry of
barcodes spreads against the seven continents,
and I am reluctant to explain to the man with
no destination where the King of Beers is.
It is not where Spotted Tail stopped at Rosebud
and Red Cloud at Pine Ridge. It is not where
the Black Hills rambled, then stopped short
in the face of Greek *logos* —
a solo flute in the night.

There are prisoners of language in Yankton
caught in a minimum wage mill. Their
fingers, their sons, their daughters are lost
and appear in plastic packaging
at supermarkets. Like puppets they dangle
and try to succeed. Like with a bad habit, they accept
the cost, and I am working like a wild symphony
late into the night so I can shop on Sunday.
*Iktomi* laughs at me in the aisles of
WalMart — if they don't have it, you don't need it.

Do you believe your gross national product?
Crazy Horse says *Hiya*. Crazy Horse
has turned to stone in South Dakota.

He talks to himself sometimes. Sometimes
he imagines he is Mozart and steps with
lighter but more confident steps.
He eats squash for lunch with a senator from
Sioux Falls who takes him to the Black Creek Inn,
three miles from highways 16 and 385.
*In the heart of the Black Hills.* Twelve units
plus cabins. M/C, Visa, Discover, AM Express.

I bring a hot dish to the sweat lodge.
Crazy Horse has never seen potatoes. We eat
off paper plates with plastic forks and knives
and then we chant for Wakan Tanka. But he
cannot appear because he is working nights
at Wendy's. It is just as well this way. His
uniform is too small, and I can't bear to see
the Great Spirit wearing double-knit. Crazy Horse
keeps adding stones, and our pores are open wide,
wailing the national anthem. After
"land of the free, home of the brave,"
I worry about fainting, my body laid out flat
on the Plains, and my spirit readying to leave me,
unable to participate in the next market survey.

## Confidences

I have trapped a moth here at the hotel in this foreign city — it is my pet.

During the day I leave the window open and let the moth bring back more stories from the city. Each night it returns with descriptions of street vendors selling grilled meat on a stick; the crowded lovers' plaza full of those who still believe in sharing passion in the daylight; a man in a straw hat sleeping underneath the palm tree where his boat is tethered, his cell phone ringing next to him.

Each night the moth returns, or at least I think it is the same moth. It would be very unsettling for me to learn I have been baring my soul each night in this little square room to a series of strange creatures floating above me from moment to moment, unsure of whether they are attracted to me or the light.

# Graça

A pleasant odor is expected of
a beautiful flower, and from bird calls
the trained ear picks out melodies.
In each case it is desire that exposes
essence. It is longing that reveals grace
moving inside of the living. My heart ticks
away, and I choose to be among the birds
and flowers without asking myself what
I need from them. I have trained myself
to be in a fight with quick gratification here
in these mountains of Espirito Santo where
hundreds of hummingbirds swarm all
around me. The pamphlet from the
museum says there are over sixty species,
emptying twenty feeders every two hours.
They light in the trees throughout
the grounds or drink the nectar of their
favorite red *graças*. I need them to teach me
about impulse. They hover and dart to
the next flower. Then a blur down the trail
and out of sight. I listen for the intervals,
passages phrased in the distant trees,
the drone of my breath as sole accompaniment.
But the bus back to Vitória leaves in
half an hour and I turn to go. I hear a buzz
rush past my ear, another one, but I see
nothing. They are grace notes and gone.
And instantly I feel fear trickle down
and collect in a place that sustains me
as I wonder what it might be like to be
shot through the heart by a hummer.

# The Ecstatic Grover

10, 9, 8, 7, 6, 5, 4, 3, 2, 1 . . .

1.        A child can learn to grope along the walls in
the dark to find the place where he confesses to
the ecstatic, where she is wedded to bliss.
Together they came to the garden of controlled
substances, the group therapies, the improved habits
grown out of trances. I, for example, was held
deeply still by Sesame Street characters, the shape
of Ernie's face, Bert's ridiculous proboscis.
Cookie Monster, that lovable but obnoxious rogue.
Each puppet is a type found all around the world.
Charles de Gaulle was Oscar. Kofi Annan is
Kermit. Julie Andrews is Big Bird. This is
the only identity test I've ever needed, and so it
shall be your measure. Are you a Snuffleupagus?
an Elmo? a Count von Count? a Guy Smiley?
I am one with Grover. I am one with Grover.

2.        [*To be read aloud in the voice of Grover*]
The home burns down to the black nub of a man's thumb.
It kills the cells that measure a bull charging as it thinks.
Its truth radiates through the eternity of species, through
the clouded heads of pines that open their cones to the tune
of a blind wind blowing pollen into the sun and steering
the force of its one true vision.

3.        A blue piece of shaggy fur for a mitt, I try to make
my hand talk to my cereal. The cereal doesn't
listen. It doesn't talk back, but there is always TV.
My puppet hand asks Luis a question at
The Fix-it Shop, and then she enters,
delivering a thump to my nine-year-old heart:
           *Maria. I've just met a girl named Maria.*
           *And suddenly that name*
           *can never be the same to me.*
           *Maria. Maria.*
Maria, why do your eyes glisten so when you recite
the alphabet to me? I watch you come alive
and let you teach me things I already know.
just one more joyous hair toss and I will
play one-of-these-things-is-not-like-the-other

46

forever. With you in the room, my puppet
drowns. The cereal is still there, the same
granola has kept appearing for years,
and now here, Maria, you have a daughter.
Your smile is still a wild flower, but
oh, Maria, why did you cut your hair?

4.        [*To be read aloud in the voice of Grover*]
A dense green races into the crowd of senses, like a body
blow, like a wingbeat on asphalt, like the fall of an ancient
doom. The living dine with the dead. Song and dance twist
on the stem of drama where overseas the graves of
airstrips burst open a perfectly preserved shadow,
their bright hope moving over the sand. And for reason:
there are contracts shared and taken into the water and
renewed.

5.        Ecstasy hides quietly in the shambles
of my life. It is my favorite appliance
in the kitchen, sparingly used on holidays
and special occasions. Widely available as
a pill, it floods serotonin and alters vision.
Running fingers through the hair is
intensely pleasurable, but I distrust pleasure.
I may be dumb or I may be innocent,
unable to give in to the experience.
It's hard for me to start right up and
jump in. This caution corners me
in a white room and makes me confess
I have lost my access to ecstasy,
the kind that used to let me laugh
uncontrollably in public, the kind I wonder
if it has abandoned me in a humorless
age. Or am I too uptight and miss it?
I wonder if Super Grover will come to
the rescue and sing a duet with me:
               *I'm fuzzy and blue*
               *You see I'm fuzzy and blue*
               *Yeah me, I'm happy to be*
               *so fuzzy and blue*
As I take this song to heart, I've learned
my happiness is directly proportional to
the number of times a day I throw my voice.

6.      [*To be read aloud in the voice of Grover*]
The skull is buried by three hours of scanning to find a fix
of oxygen. A vision barrels along the river of critical
thinking, two samples of salt water. They call these
fountains *ojos de agua*. A huge amount of dead matter
floats between the herds and the songs of the herders.
A flute says goodbye to its sunless household.

My wife comes home and chides me,
*Honey, you need a happiness makeover.* I've been
stuck the last few days like a copier with
the error light blinking. I cannot lift my eyes
up to another, nor any time soon. I should
train myself like a puppy to respond to
my generation's praise for things I do not
understand, the expediency of thought and
phrase, the permanent vacation, the warm glow
of disposable cash in hand. Long is the road
to anhedonia. I am driven there by my master,
serotonin, who hints at reappearing like
a tired god. Oh Lord Serotonin, this hole
you make me sleep in, it gives me a back ache.
My back aches and my perspective distorts.
I cannot get started for the life of me.
But without you neither can a cat or dog.
On its walk a cocker spaniel freezes and you
abandon it, vanishing to a trace, a flicker.
The cocker spaniel moves forward and you
surge to the wagging tail and the moving feet.
You are my motivation by another name
that tracks my halting speech, attracts me
to the polar barrens of despondency.
I throw my voice at another age to throw off
my blind anger at this one, my innocence
and ecstasy broken off and fed bit by bit
to all the hungry birds. I lost the game of
serotonin uptake with my peers, and I
blame you Maria, Why did you cut
your goddamned beautiful hair?

7.      [*To be read aloud in the voice of Grover*]
A man grew up on Granite Street with his camera peeking at
the decades to come, at the cemetery of ferns where all
speech ends as boom and bust overflowing the attention
span. A recital of white noise empties into the back lot

where these intense minutes are held under a storm.

8.        I cannot speak with contractions anymore
        as part of my formal training to be Grover.
        I am enrolled in the intense school of proper
        speech where a dropped g at the end of
        a gerund means I'm in a slump again.
        But who needs Prozac when there are
        puppets in the house? I slip on Jocko
        the monkey and commence my hero's journey
        to find bliss surfing through the network
        news shows. The world is crumbling,
        superstitious, in an advanced stage of
        suspicion, unwilling to risk a trial
        of herbal remedies. I hurl epithets at
        the anchorman's face. I'm a stream of
        ad hominem. I am the critical American
        who has divorced that word from its
        partner word — thinking. Am I trying
        too hard to be happy, to make myself feel
        better, or am I trying too hard to make
        my voice sound like a monkey's?
        Jocko rests on my hand, and I try to
        speak to the tragic world directly,
        but my lips barely move, unable to
        fully get started as I return again
        to my hallucinations while watching
        Sesame Street.

9.        [*To be read aloud in the voice of Grover*]
        The cancer of personality disturbs the abyss. At first
        human beings lasted all night long like a personal belief.
        Fidelity to the body was needed; barley and wheatgrass
        brush against a Nebraska starkly tended, hidden in the wild
        maze of the cerebrum's fissures. A clay horse resists
        a pasture. Its patience rests in the private waters that settle in
        a puddle.

1, 2, 3, 4, 5, 6, 7, 8, 9 . . .

10.      The statistics on happiness are not
        very happy. Anti-depressants rank
        below any anti-ulcers and anti-cholesterols.
        Dog and cat owners are no happier
        than the petless. Evangelicals *are*

happier than those who sleep late
on Sunday. Everyone knows that
numbers lie, even the simple
counting ones. This morning I heard
Maria counting them out loud again
and faking her enthusiasm.
Her verve impresses me, bewilders
me in its foreign feel. I can only
consider how the whole fortunate
ball of appetites rolls forward,
motivated at the molecular level.
I keep spinning around the bliss of
the sun invested on my behalf
in chlorophyll ways and means.
I have failed its remedial course
in being, but the sun keeps giving
and giving, turning me into
a relic of happiness past.

[*To be sung aloud in the voice of Grover*]
    *I'm fuzzy and blue*
    *You see I'm fuzzy and blue*
    *Yeah me, I'm happy to be*
    *so fuzzy and blue*

# Lutheran Prayer

I am serious. I repent. Sins stock
the shelves alongside all the ordinary
career plans. I call Mr. Fix-it to
reconstruct my life — from the
beginning. No. Starting halfway through.
Halfway through my life I am finding
enough time to rethink what has
happened to me. This rethinking is
serious business and a Lutheran
God is nowhere in sight. I pray for the
dead weight of my family to anchor me
and hope I can imagine the rest.

# The Undertaker's Sale

I bought back my childhood from an undertaker.
He had tried it on like a fool tries on underwear.
I offered him all my ambitions; he left me empty,
a father of two whose needs surfaced and vibrated
like bathtub toys. I played. Again, I wore my childhood,
but the leg holes stretched too big. Undertakers!
I finally found him, pinning my hopes on the dead.

# The Ease of Preference

I go to the market to absorb the confidence of
the melons. They are thick, luminous, full of juice and
seeds. Their smell works a room like the smile of
a charismatic felon. But I find myself the only one at
the display table of chayote. They are the burn victims
everyone shies away from. I try to ease their doubt by
touching their blistered skin. Drying out slowly,
they serve as icons of the grotesque, immune to
the negotiations going on around them.
The market crowd pinches itself into frenzied clusters,
everyone trying to get the next good deal,
the one certain to be mentioned in casual conversation.
I will tell you of the gains made every time I go.
I will grab for apples, sample raspberries,
each time knowing it's sweeter to get what I want
instead of what I deserve.

# The Sense on the Streets

The sense on the streets is the rainy season is coming.
A man stops and asks me if I like the rain.
I expand upon its many qualities, weigh several
mitigating factors, explain a variety of past experiences.
The man stops me, asks *Can't you give me a straight answer?*
*No*, I respond, *why do you expect one?*
I tell him there are no such things as
preferences fossilized in this hunk of hamburger
I masquerade in. Situations arise, and I respond
like an obedient student asked to recite the Pledge
of Allegiance. The man looks at me like I'm a moral
imbecile. Our meeting is too brief for me to assure
him I'm not, that I've been diligently working
on a plan to teach my students how to deal with
the most common form of *weltschmerz*. They come to
class with their puka shells on and leave shouldering
a small but menacing burden. I cannot say how long
they will let the situation of the world nag them.
I cannot say how many times they will give up,
then begin again. *It's hard work* I confide to them,
like building a nation on the grounds of compassion.
Yet it is the only way to move off the starting line.
*Go, let the group hugging begin* I implore them,
just as I am winning them over, but the sense on
the streets is that standing around in the rain
hugging someone is a ridiculous idea. The sense
on the streets is the rainy season is coming from
somewhere. We should all go home now immediately,
a little cloud following each of us there.

# Black Rock

The small, black rock you sent is here with me. I am looking at its profile, trying to get a reading on how its plies are stuck together. They look like they could be pried apart, one ply peeled away from the other the way a lapel can be peeled away from a dark suit to reveal torn felt beneath the collar. I wonder if I peeled them apart would I miss the perfectly oval shape of the rock that the river has painstakingly carved for me? Would I be nostalgic for its pure form as I have become for the petals of the blue hydrangea I planted on Mother's Day, now slowly withering?

It is obvious the black rock has been dealt with violently, smashed. It is the stain of a dark fecal pellet that one might find at the bottom of a cage of a neglected animal. The animal has not seen the sun for fourteen days and it might already be dead even as we speak of it, curled up in the newspaper which has printed the news of a war where black rocks fall out of the sky and are smeared across the faces of intrepid onlookers, smeared like some kind of horrible scarring dark rouge, so permanent that, like deep hopeless sleep, it must be beautiful.

And I swallow the small black rock, today's horsepill, to shake down some meaning from the celestial fruit trees in heaven. The routine of making substance vanish is meaningful: so many things disappear from sight momentarily. Yet I trust they are still there. I move them mentally into the category of "something missing." So far from the river where it came from, the black rock passes through me, and I am afraid of the outcome. Will my hackle shed? Will I catch and tear on someone I run into? I can spend the next few moments on the lessons these thoughts teach me, contemplating the inertia of loss. And then all that remains is survival which depends on my being porous enough to let the dark fall through.

# Crusade

Someone was running all around the house
killing all the flies, leaving their smashed
corpses out in plain view. I asked everyone
I knew "Who is doing this?" The neighbor
to the east said "I don't know, but it happened
to me too." The neighbor to the west brought tea
to calm me and told me she saw some men crawling
through my window. There was a madman
running through my house ridding it of filth and
vermin. In the yard there was evidence of
fresh graves. The cobwebs in the highest corners
of the vaulted ceilings were missing. I didn't
hear scurrying behind the baseboards any longer.
I tried to think of how peaceful the nights would be,
how clean the floors were, cleaner than I could ever
remember them. I didn't want to touch anything;
I took pictures to show the authorities. And when they
arrived, I vehemently complained about how I had been
violated by the intruders, but they only seemed to care
if any valuables were missing. And they puzzled over
why the perpetrators hadn't completed their mission.
There were dead flies on all the furniture, in the sinks
and closets, behind the drapes, on ledges, underneath
the refrigerator. Complete strangers came in to look at
them and shake their heads in wonder at why
the exterminators had hurried so at the end and left
things unfinished. Perhaps there had been good reasons
at the start and then they ran out of them.
Perhaps they had used up all their passion.
And I looked down on all the scattered corpses
for clues. I looked into their compound eyes, but
all I could see were the imprints of so many empty motives.

# Headspin Sandwich

In Chicago I ate a sandwich for lunch, and my head spun like a dervish's. My eyes tried to crawl up the wall of the deli and catch on all the delights on the counter, but my eyes kept slipping, falling onto the linoleum. I could not stand up. My wallet was heavy. The words in the newspaper confused me, and I started to feel sick. Then the music, like the soft music piped into men's bathrooms. The lights were turned down low, and I spun as the room grew dim.

I spun and spun, heading east into the past — New York, London, Paris, Vienna, Zagreb, Kiev, Beijing. There to the right of me were the future children of silk merchants, to the left, the discarded wisdom of Lao Tzu who was pressing down desire with an uncarved block.

I washed my face in a puddle. The wet and its simple charm. There might be days ahead without food. There might be no change of clothes, no photographs to recall, no examinations of a life that is better. There is nothing to imagine except the needs of others and nothing I can do to buy my way free.

# Heliocracy

I cannot remark on the colors of the dawn or why
it resorts to ventriloquism. The day speaks truths as it
warms over. I sit, sweat and watch the colors hatch
out of the morning, each in a stage of drying on
the litter of objects sprawled in the sun. I pick up a
rock and let the sun talk through it. The words wear
a stillness disguise. But there are other ways to catch
a glimpse of the words flying off the tongue
of a rock. Pretend the rock is not even there.
Observe the dust trailing off in the wind
in the direction the conversation has ventured.
A rock has the guile to go unnoticed, and
even if watched carefully, it still looks stupid.
But it is steady. Steadiness is
the way it lives out its dreams,
and anything that dreams must be sentient.
They have sympathy for us humans,
so I used to feel I had to say nice things about
the rocks. It was like they were primates. I was
continually looking sideways at them, hoping
for some insight into their nature. I would often
think a rock does not have impulses,
but I was mistaken. An avalanche is a slur
of guttural vowel sounds; a volcano, a shout at the moon.
If one drops a rock on the sidewalk, it utters
the code of its life in a flash of quick, short
syllables. Still, the consensus is that rocks are thought
to be mute, and this is why for many years rocks
were seen as excellent pets. They spoke very little,
and when they did speak, it was usually
the sun with its big brain talking through them.
The sun has its way with everything.
You cannot tell what it is thinking. It can turn a
gray stone white. The sun will make you forget
your name. Then you will dream like a rock or
a tangled-up puppet and feel lucky the world happens
as quietly as it does. The silence repeats itself.
The silence folds evenly over the morning. The silence
layers the colors at dawn over the hidden life of
everything, but sometimes one is able to tell if the rocks
have received their orders to march on steadfastly,
espousing the tranquil philosophy of the sun.

# Hominid Love Letter

The shape of your femur suggests that you woke up
each day with a destination on your mind while I
was aimless and scavenged for deer, never knowing
if I would bring it back to the cave for you, my dear.
I never knew the child was mine either, so I stuck to
scraping hides in my hovel with the other men . . .
And now they tell me, this is why we Neanderthals
are buried with our memories and hopes. And you,
Homo sapiens who paired and mated are credited
with birthing the imagination. But let me tell you there
are times now in my dark home when I can picture
your slender body, your sweet chin, your compressed pelvis
that seemed as dense as a flat rock to pound on. And I
wonder why you chose a man with such great brow ridges
like me who needed a shave and a good set of clothes.
I want to know why you took me in your arms so sweetly,
without displaying, and let my thick, coarse body
be forgiven again and again and again. I want to know why
you loved me, my dear. This question may seem stupid
to you after so many years, after our child has grown
and gone to swirl its genes among all these modern humans,
but I am looking for an answer. I need to know why
I am not such a pitiable thing. I need to know why
I am not beyond redemption. I need to know that
I am human even though I regret our home life was
not like the other humans whom you know.
Please tell this dumb creature. I need to know why
you loved me, dear. So, I have learned these words
to ask you this here where I am now, in the dark,
aimless, wandering within this ultimate privacy
of mine where I am nothing and you are the future
I have dreamed.

# Signal-to-Noise Ratio

So gifted was he in the *art* of language,
the vice president of marketing for the Brazilian
steel firm could not tell me what the noun and
verb were in the sentence he was using.
Nor could he say the same for any sentence,
and I was the brash, young American teacher
pointing out this deficiency. Perhaps this lack
of his was meaningless, like a parrot's inability to
gargle or recite "The Road Not Taken" from memory.
He had no time for such stupid tricks, these little
affectations of mind, when he was charged with
the task of selling, of knowing the needs and
interests of others through knowing his own.
Through the noise and chatter of his life,
the cell phone conversations lost to
muffle and static, he had learned the power
of the male human heart decreases with age.
So it is better to love young out of habit
than to wonder later if it can be done at all
like my old friend who calls drunk and rambling
late into the night about the Spanish lovers
he lost, the girl in Mexico whom he could marry,
if he got her papers in order. He talks on his
cell phone for hours from a bar in Denver,
rehearsing one lover's bedridden silence that
exploded into accusation — how he took the best
years of her life . . . without asking for them.
He can't ask me outright for help, either,
so he becomes the drunken narrator, reciting
his broken memories, unable to locate his life's
constituent parts that might enable him to
reach completion. After all these years,
he got my number off a database. He had millions
of names to choose from, all that human confusion
out there coded in numbers without error.
But when mistakes are made, identities get misplaced,
distorted. The wires hum with data leakage.
I can't effectively decide what kind of American
I want to be, and if I do decide,
there's a host of problems with transmission.
I can pulse in a sheen of pheromones,
one more animal with protocol for propagation

that invents an artful story on the spot
or enters into a prolonged negotiation with one.
The past insists "story" is a noun;
the future believes it must be verb.

# The Land of Opportunity

for Jane Dark

*It's not unusual to be loved by anyone.*
*It's not unusual to have fun with anyone.*
But I would never begin to assume that anyone
would ever critique a flower or would ever find the notion
of a modern nation to be a death by slow waltz.
It's not unusual for a culture to seek commerce
in labels, the broad back of a name or word burdened
with a segregating edge that expands
the material process of class. I, for example, belong
to a group of verb abusers. Membership depends
on ignoring the past tense, and then we sing about
markets as a many wormholed foam. The selves slide
down into their chambers, locked and loaded
and ready to explode into a sky that has
already been paid for, hanging loosely
above the land of opportunity.

**Gurtmuffel.** [(n.) German] — someone who doesn't wear a seat belt

> Critical thinking is motivated by the effort to transcend the tension
> and to abolish the opposition between the individual's purposeful
> ness, spontaneity, and rationality, and those work-process relation
> ships on which society is built.
> — Max Horkheimer

I play a game with my 6- and 8-year-old sons called fruit farts.
The object is to say the name of the fruit after contained bowel gases
have become more diffuse. The last one to say "apple" or "plum" or
"apricot" is then said to be visited by "the curse of the stench." But
the game quickly devolves into routine. The names of fruits are uttered
under false pretenses. Exclaiming "apple" or "mango" or "grapefruit"
signals neither alert nor does it serve as protective spell against the
unpleasant odors. In fact, after a while, it is difficult to determine whose
words mark an authentic release.

In the land of opportunity everyone is an opportunist.
There are squirrels jumping inside of baby strollers and
searching for bags of food. At the Ripley's Believe-It-Or-Not Museum
a man kisses a cobra nineteen times to set a world record.
In the land of opportunity hermit crabs are often in the market for

a new shell. They tap, tap, tap, tap, to measure the size of the other like the play between those two historical puppets, Punch and Judy, who despite every opportunity raised as the target spouse for the other, failed to ever have sexual relations, *but if you should ever want to be loved by anyone. It's not unusual. It happens every day. No matter what you say.* You find it happens when the mind is reorganized to forever sever the ties between work, rest, and play. Then the following Tuesday in another tidy domain of the mind poetry meets critical theory and karaoke.

**Handschuhschneeballwerfer.** [(n.) German] — someone who wears gloves to throw snowballs.

My two sons are playing kitties again on a pile of blankets the way I played Charlie the Lonesome Cougar with my babysitter who appeased me by pretending to give me meat. Was I only seeking opportunity the way my sons do by rubbing against their mother and meowing for an after-dinner treat? *Meow* for ice cream. *Meow Meow* for a chocolate chip cookie. But they don't meow at me. Am I missing my felinity? Have I moved on to exclude and be excluded, that middle class game that always makes me feel as if I'm going to be the first to get kicked out of the middle class because of my flare-ups of apathy towards it.

> Bourgeois thought is essentially abstract and its principle is an
> individuality which inflatedly believes itself to be the ground of
> the world or even to be the world without qualification,
> an individuality separated off from events.
> — Max Horkheimer

**Geisterfahrer.** [(n.) German] — someone who drives the wrong way down the Autobahn.

*What's New, Pussycat? Whoa Whoa*
Oh, Tom Jones, you are that everyman who dances naked in front
of the mirror
        of nature.
You are the tallest sunflower in the region. You are the noise level
underwater in the ocean
        increasing every day.
Oh, Tom Jones, you are the sexual revolution reconstituted by adding
water. You are the
        campaign to eliminate the hopeless wish for love, the wish
that beats down the formal
        logic of pricing.
You are a quantity of attempted feats organized into artless
categories. You are the labor of dying

bees, pollinators of hill flowers and roses trashed on busy
roads. You are the fuel of drifting speech.
Oh, Tom Jones, you are a Gurtmuffel, a Geisterfahrer. I am Tom Jones,
too, but that is not
unusual. Oh, Tom Jones, you belong to that class of words
for which there is no noun.
Only the verbs review how to subvert and rout the enemy
for which there is no
lasting profile. There is no instrument of faith beyond the
infinite wall of sound that is
Tom Jones singing:
*love de love de loo*
*what you wanna do?*
*why can't this crazy love be mine?*
Why can't this crazy love be mired in a culture of commerce
with its labels displayed on packages, on stamps and stickers,
on the underside of furniture, deep in the guts of machines?
Are there no words left that deliver a moment together,
carved from a spontaneous riff, an accent mark over the oeuvre
that carries the juices of you and me and the one and only,
the original Tom Jones forward into the authentic?
The nouns there are pollinated by the verbs.
The words and names are muffled and emptied,
stripped of the classifications they have signaled
until . . . the following Tuesday when the next "best deal"
is offered in the land of opportunity,
the land of opportunity, where everyone is an opportunist.

# III.

Why do you gaze at the distant city?
Your soul is the distant city.
It rains a chill rain.

— Fernando Pessoa

# Sort and Accumulate

What is the gist of a dark indifference, of a colorless
cloudy day? Can a thought extend beyond the wind through
the heather? I search the bric-a-brac and specimens
at Goodwill for answers, for my answer to
Alvaro de Campos's tremors of inadequacy.
I resurrect him from the piles of clothes.
Is there anything more useful, more important than
the ability to sort? The socks and bras get tied together,
and they need my labor to separate them, the way I can separate
de Campos from his others — naïve Caeiro offering
the natural egoism of flowers, Reis recalling himself from afar.
I see you, Fernando Pessoa, your hat in a bin mixed with
barbershop quartet records, the harmonies thick but
each part distinct. I see you, Pessoa, dreading
the memories returning to you in these things,
your recollections of the mysterious silence of Lisbon,
your home. My town has a river running through it,
and a man here buys an old typewriter, carries it
under his arm on his bike. Is that you riding over the tracks
and heading south to type out an ode? Whose name does
the river give to you today as it wanders from grip to grip?
You instinctively seem to be rehearsing its form.
I might see you twice, once in a crowd at a charity event,
again, disguised on the sidelines at a soccer match in the park.
Is that you once more, a little boy fishing and listening to
hip-hop? The tide off the coast of Lisbon has swept you up
and suddenly transformed you into an overprescribed American,
struggling to remain true to your failing and singular body.
I should spend some time with you, share a bowl of soup,
and reveal the deeply ingrained flow of personality in you,
you know, the one everyone keeps track of in themselves,
but I have too damn many personalities of my own.
I have unconsciously initiated a pattern that always leads
to the self as obstacle, something prepared for me to
climb over and exercise my heart. I launch myself over
and around the decades past, the decades to come,
the trial balloons rising up and away from me, each with
a different magic-markered face. They rise to mimic the faces
in the clouds on all these colorless days when Americans feel
wounded in the world and are having trouble making
the best of it. Then, they turn to the face of the consumer
and let the massage of the advertiser's guile begin.

Let the 30-second spots and aisles of discounts replenish
spirits, let the mock-ups at Home Depot serve as
temptations. I wonder why I always see you, Caeiro,
picking out the straightest lumber. There is something
reaffirming in this, right? Don't answer. I don't expect
a sensate poet who only sees the world to reveal himself.
Nor can I explain why the classicist Reis who can't find
steel electrical boxes settles for the PVC plastic.
Only you do I understand, de Campos, who wastes
his life roaming the merchandise to discover something
universal about the human condition. The facts of
existence dictate men are fastened with screwdrivers,
scraps of wire, and duct tape. They wear their ragged clothes
found in the bins at Goodwill forever, with an exaggerated
indifference to the dead and the bored and the extravagant
who wore them beforehand. Whose dark occupation
is it to sort out the names still left on the tags, clinging
to their former owners? Am I the only anthropologist
of American excess? When I find a mirror in the heap,
who will appear there—Reis, de Campos, Pessoa, Caeiro?
Some other lurker in a borrowed wardrobe? I know I should
pass myself off as one who buzzes around and does
a half dozen good deeds before lunch. I might fix a broken
laptop, return it to its genuine state, but that can never happen.
Nothing repaired is ever pristine. Nothing touched up
can hold its face the same. I can photoshop my eyes, ears,
mouth, and nose to look like some vacant searcher.
The elements of me, morphed and pixeled, dispersing
like a talented wind through the heather. I can be run
through the bins, sorted and sampled, until I earn
my degree of other. Why do you ride shotgun with me
again, de Campos? Are we going to Goodwill once more?
Thrown clear by the market's pressures, we are free
to remake what we find there. All of it might otherwise
seem useless. It inspires a dark indifference. So why do you
keep ghosting me as if there were something else
I should find and keep? All I really need to know
is what I want; then I can be an American.

# To Live Enough

The morning sun slaps me with purpose,
and in America that means I should be
competing somewhere. But I am analyzing
the news come from afar and making no progress,
witness to another moral vacuum,
dark clots of desire thickening here and there.

I push myself to ask what's wrong with
wanting, that little pinprick of the flesh
that keeps everyone moving in the morning,
but in America the word heaps: it means
wanting too much. I ask the empty branch
of the apricot why it should want to live enough.

The mouth of a busy robin answers.
I hurry off to school with my two sons.
A mother tells me she is holding her son
back from starting kindergarten,
another year before he learns
how to do what must be done.

I could tell her that the markets will
punish him, but I don't want my story
to influence her decision. She hails from
Mexico City, and I let her America soak
into me. Time for analysis later,
when my winnings are
bleached and burned by the sun.

# Adequacy

One morning my wife earnestly tells me
she's thankful I'm so darned adequate.
She means this as a compliment,
that in some small but measurable ways
I've actually improved. But I'm not ready
to concede that up until now I've been failing.
Just because I prefer drinking from
a dirty glass doesn't mean I can't be
exceptional. It doesn't mean I'm
dedicated to being shabby.
And just because I think a second pot
of coffee with the same grounds
is perfectly good, this is not a reason
to believe I would put mud in a strainer
and call the water that ran through it
a tonic. I have realized, after many
false impressions, the world is a decent
place to be because everything works
well enough. Cogs mesh and forces balance.
If this is something called adequacy,
then let its presence span every
fence between neighbors and every nation's
borders. Let each excursion into
a disputed orchard turn out OK.
The fruit that falls to the ground will be
used in bread-making. Those precious moments
of feeling uniquely alive will continue to be
satisfactory. I will adjust my enthusiasm
as my wife admits she is proud of me.
She is proud because I've learned to be
as concerned as the next average Joe
about those who look down on my existence.

# A Wisdom Fable

A woman gives me a book that speaks of
the world as an intersection of dreams.
It is the philosophy of a man who
uses only one blanket when he sleeps.
And while he sleeps, he dreams that
he believes nothing — that there are
no mistakes, no judgments, no victims
of guilt. There is only the one blanket
covering everything. It is a blanket of
awakening instinct. Alas, the world
is a movie with no speaking parts, and
the actors all sleep as they impulsively lurch
in the middle of their unrehearsed scenes.

I dream about the book for twelve days.
Every night a million people are
talking, but none of them understand
one another. They are talking hurriedly,
like they are just remembering something they
used to be afraid of and they must speak
before it begins haunting them again.
The woman who gave me the book is
among them. She is naked from the waist
down. She keeps telling me that
I should do only what I want to do.

But waking up is my first responsibility.
I must read the next few pages to see
how I can finally accept wisdom. I will need
it now more than ever since I have had
my vasectomy. These are the days of
sluggishness, of no belief in anything —
no mistakes, no judgments, no nagging feelings
of guilt. There would be a simple peace
if only I could get my wife to agree with
my new but determined hopelessness.

Now she is reading this same book too,
but she won't tell me what she's dreaming.
I must try to read her mind over
Sunday morning coffee. She is good at
this game and easily outwits me.

She thinks of nothing, but it is a different
nothing than the one I am committed to.
She seems vapid and contented, so much so
that I am jealous, and I imagine us lying
together, mute in the silence under one
large blanket. We appear lifeless,
like we have somehow learned to inhabit
the pristine wisdom of a cadaver.
The air instinctively gathers us in its coils,
and we feel along its smooth muscles, its
racing pulse until we touch the soft ground,
ecstatic, ready to cross over into
the empty realm of each other's dream.

# Tupperware

At our first Tupperware party together it suddenly hits my wife
        and me
that we don't know anybody who is separated. We are comparing
        storage capacities and
locking mechanisms. Women are leafing through bright catalogs.
        The men are discussing
places where traffic in the city tends to snarl. These couples
        don't remind us of anybody
we knew in college. At that time we hung out in gangs of a
        single gender. We paired off,
two by two, almost accidentally, then headed off for distant cities
        together.

When we returned one weekend, we saw some friends from
        college get married after years
of doubt and anticipation. For years they had seemed unable to
        show the requisite enmity
married people must show towards single people. But after years
        of living together, they were
finally able to express some pity for the poor, unmarried souls
        walking up and down the strip,
looking for someone in the windows of the cafes, the bars and
        upstairs apartments,
hoping for that instant of eye contact which would launch their
        future.

Our old friends got married in the park. Afterwards, my wife and
        I watched a group of
families around the picnic tables. We wondered which couples
        belonged to each other,
mixing and matching as we went, the possibilities leading to other
        possibilities that suggested
any man and any woman could be better off with or without each
        other. And then last week, the woman
who is always talking about her son, Miguel, calls me to tell me
        she has left some old baby clothes
with Miguel's father. *Miguel's father?* I ask her to clarify. She was
        heading back to Madison
that morning for the sake of her son, for her mother, dying of
        cancer. She was turning herself
out of the club of married people. She was heading out on the
        road to worry.

And there we would be the following week among all the
                couples at our first Tupperware party
together. We would be driving home loaded down with
                Tupperware samples, trying to imagine
what they might hold. We would try to imagine the freshness of
                his and hers leftovers
sitting on the cool shelves of the refrigerator safe from spoilage
                and contamination.
We might imagine the way home, the path that brought us here,
                the future we were throwing
ourselves headlong into. The baby in the car seat would be
                wearing his new clothes permanently on loan
from Miguel's mother. I could lean over to my wife and whisper
                — *Well, now that we got*
*all this Tupperware I guess we're stuck with each other.* And we might
                guess that as people's lives
spill over each other, the only thing we can do is to let the
                accidents happen, contain them, and then
try to pry the lid off and marvel at how quickly things go rotten
                at the center.

# Mail File

Every day something comes in the mail
that I can use as a bookmarker. I can lose
notices of upcoming sales between the pages
of ancient world history. A flood of ads marks
my progress through the works of Shakespeare.
Letters from friends hold vigil in
the Swedish dictionary. And the novels
on my shelf wait for coupons to become
lodged among the mysteries of the words
held captive in them. The mail arrives
and joins me near my library where
I have lost my way along a trail of written
treasures that grows more and more
treacherous without any little slips of
paper to help me find my way back to
where I've been. The atlas is useless
in such instances. A map is superfluous
when you travel through time, back
through centuries of gossip to dig up
an old crop of adages and pass them along
in the next letter sent. And when the letter
reaches its destination, the reader will
take the time to note the postmark
even though the printed date in no way
reflects its age. The words of the dead tend
to wander, yet they still make good neighbors,
living here for years in my library on lots
that have been marked off painstakingly by
the little flags of paper that are their addresses.

# Dead Air

I listen to the dead air of the broadcast
on the internet during the rain delay of the Cubs,
a few stubborn fans let out a whoop over Waveland.
The thunder cracks its warning that calms me.
I miss those Midwest summer storms since I've been
stationed in the summer Central Valley heat,
drying out like a prune, passing blood and stones
in my urine. I listen to the rain tap dance on the seats
near where the mics have been left up.
It's anybody's guess whether they'll resume play.
Who cares? It's Wrigley. There's always next year,
and the years after that when my brother
hopes to come back in the next life as
a Marin County terrier. Another brother nearly
realizes his life's ambition — to die in battle.
This time it's with his wife, and after it's over
he professes: *there are many rooms in the doghouse.*
A third brother has solved the problem of
global warming — mass extermination. Make me king,
and we'll start with the Yankees and their fans,
then the Red Sox, the White Sox, maybe the whole
American League. Then we decimate the Cardinals
while my brothers and I sing the victory song
        *Go Cubs Go, Go Cubs Go*
        *Hey, Chicago, whaddya say?*
        *The Cubs are gonna win today*
We'll sing it all the way into late October.
But for now there is only a drunken yell and
a lone whistle echoing off the grandstands.
The storm strafes the infield tarp.
The broadcast's dead air returns me to
the Chicago home of my youth, stuck indoors
with my three brothers listening to
the drops bomb the roof shingles.
How did our crackpot ideas become underdogs
in this unforgiving age? This age wants results,
winners. No one should be listening to the dead air
in a delayed baseball game, even if the score
is tied and the season hangs in the balance.
But the sound draws me into some damned
nostalgia, which for the moment, feels
as right as rain.

# Baptism

There is nothing to understand about
                    the satisfied smile of the garbage pickers.
A little bit of dirt under the fingernails
                    reminds me to wash my food.

Survivors throw glances at the sky
                    and give the stars their names.
Water evaporating on the forehead, wrists, and temples
                    clarifies decisions.

My thoughts are of no use to the squirrels;
                    I throw them peanuts.
Tonight I let the moss take over the bark of the oak tree.

I know my double has been drinking dark beer today.
All day long, the rain steady, the river spills over the levee.

In a city of trees, the working man treats squirrels
                    as the mind's plaything.
Three bearded men sit at the end of an offramp
                    with signs asking for money.

My tires are full of air; my windshield is clean —
                    I drive beneath
a half-moon and wish myself a name that
                    the river can wash over.

My mirror image in standing water is the same as
                    a man who picks tomatoes for a living.
January is a question, February an answer, March brings
                    more unexpected weather.

The best light to study the dark is candlelight;
                    it belongs to no one.
My name and my father's name will be given to another.

# Interpretation of Life in a Fishbowl

My son is born with one testicle.
It is sure to be recognized as a curiosity.
There will be gawkers in showers to contend with
and questions from lovers during bedroom
examinations. That's life in the fishbowl, as they say.
I stare through the glass during the hospital inspection,
hoping someday I will have something meaningful to
say to him. I have a little one-balled man who is
coming to the surface to feed on the few memories I have
sprinkled there. I remember my dad telling me
in order to be a man I had to learn to be accepting,
because at some point, I would lose something.
I think he said this because he had come through
the Depression. But now losing has another kind of
meaning that confuses me. Sometimes late at night
I wonder about this question: is my son's scrotum indeed
half-full or half-empty? I keep having a vision that
as the new millennium is ushered in, his absent testicle
will descend like the shimmering sphere that descends on
Times Square — no teeming crowds cheering it on
as it falls. There need not be any public fanfare for this
simple miracle. But for now, there is only this age-old
question of sorting the optimists from the pessimists,
a question that can only be answered in private,
in the presence of a few intimate others who have seen
a person at his best and worst, who can judge
whether a life is either half-empty or half-full
or some other curious floating animal.

# Loss of Rapture

The dog is curled up with its chew toy.
I am curled up with the dog, and next to me
my wife battles the strange opiate which keeps
her up at night unable to relinquish her duties to
the wakeful world. She can't let go into the bliss
of absence. Here she is awake, diagnosing her
troubles, sorting through the filler of her days
which have brought her to this moment
lying in the darkness, studying its chasms where,
deep within, lies joy. She will raise her haggard body
in the morning, off to repeat countless little tortures
until there seems no time left over to remember
when she could stand still with a fixed gaze in awe of
the loss of herself into rapture, then the weight
rushing back into her body and the mind's counter
resetting itself to zero, releasing her back to
the present. Now the dog is sniffing in its sleep,
running after birds and squirrels. I lash out in violent
spasms of frustration and dream away my headaches.
These are the days I should be coping, aided by
instant karma. These are the fast days where
everything gets blurry as it shoots by. I don't want
to lose focus, and I don't want to lose that thing
which is its opposite, that thing which my wife
stews over in the middle of the night as she lies
awake, that thing she thinks is passing, is lost,
not just hidden. That thing which expands calm
like a balloon full of helium, floating away
into the stratosphere's winds which blow and
blow without my knowledge of their blowing.

## Asleep at the Theme Park

I am a friend of the decaf and
all those disenfranchised by sleep at
three in the morning, like this feral
cat looking for a handout or the wide-awake
night watchman protecting me from
nameless harm. The hotel doors are locked
so that I am free to believe, without
distraction, in my own catharsis.
I can load myself with a grotesque pity
as the night advances in age.
Oh, sleep, don't let me labor anymore,
eating Froot Loop after Froot Loop.
I have studied the golf map of San Diego,
compared boat rental brochures,
watched a war film marketed to
the generation after me.
Tomorrow I go to the theme park.
I will stand in line at the rides
like the other zombies, forced to
subsist on starchy foods and
the idea that we are doing something
to benefit our children. I fear
falling asleep before the day is over,
not present at the moment they decide
whether their heroes will be cartoon
characters or exotic animals, still asleep
when they decide whose theme they will
be imagining next week or a year
from now when on an ordinary morning,
I will wake up, soberly carrying my
coffee cup across the room, as they
hide from sight in their fort of
many blankets draped across the chairs
and transform me into the dangerous and
hideous monster from the film
they carefully watched the night before.

# Black Widow During Spring Cleaning

The dead body was resting on the kitchen counter

like a demigod forced to share a bed.

My sons observed the red hourglass on its abdomen,

its death an act of submission to the notion

of order. I admit to playing the part of

hero heading up the safety awareness commission,

clearly laying out the dangers for children

who are tired of admonishments.

"Isn't it beautiful?" I asked them. A corpse is

the loneliest form of expression. It has nothing to

share but its presence, and now I have just been handed

this update: there is no safety in numbers.

The black head of malice could sweep by and kiss

all of us out of sympathy for its version of heaven.

# Phallocrypt

I decide to run naked on the Slip 'n Slide in my backyard,
my wife warning me about head and neck injuries.
My two sons bare all as well, genitals flailing like
miniature wings. My wife warns that the neighbors
in the two-story can see over the fence and tell
who has been circumcised and who hasn't. But we are
a little tribe of suburbanites, unfazed by who is
gawking at us, like the Dani tribesmen of New Guinea,
whose phallocrypts must endure a thousand tourists'
photographs. They believe birds and humans once
lived together. They have words for only two colors.
They are great models for us who are trying to simplify
our lives, who are still a little confused by
all the publicity given to private matters
and all the influence given to men who wear the pants.

# The Destructo Years

I find the glass ornament broken in the trash;
the ball's bladder, eviscerated, lying on the sidewalk,
hopes a medic will find it. Every pencil in the house
has had its eraser decapitated. Their points are
broken off, smashed, cracked, splintered.
I have a ready stock of wooden shivs.
The gouge in the drywall is the shape of
my mother's face in profile. Oh, dear mother,
why didn't you warn me before you died?
Why didn't you warn me about
the destructo years — that age in a young boy's life
when his physical strength is tested against
the structural integrity of every solid object.
Did my three brothers and I drive you
to your grave? Were you the force
we strained against until your heart crumpled
like a beer can crushed underfoot in
a parking lot? And now that the world
has beaten my brothers and me down —
jobless, diseased, underemployed, suspicious
of everyone's greed — what invisible strength
keeps us from destroying our lives any further?
What remains is useful. I want to use
the scraps I find to build a working model
of a patient mother. But I'm not so certain
it can be done. This simple imagined task
keeps breaking down in my head.
I forget how my feats of strength harmed
the silverware, my shoes, the stubborn
wind-up clock whose every tick
annoyed me and seemed to warn
someday I would inherit my trash.

## Missing the Leonids

Standing on the roof early in the morning
and peering into the empty cabinet of the sky,
I count on the trail of comet debris to amaze me,
the meteors streaking through the atmosphere
to blink and flare like red-eye flights for Fresno
strung up between the fixture stars. The city to
the north is shining too boldly. The technicolored
feats of light are obscured by clouds and haze.
In a hundred or so Novembers the lights
will concede to being a spectacle again.
Tomorrow night the constellations will hold still
for me, and my eyes will resume their queries.
So much goes on behind the curtain that I
will never see. Is it integrity or stubbornness
that keeps the night sky so modest?

I was an adolescent with a middle part
when Kohoutek last graced the night stage.
When Halley's came, I was an undergraduate
playing quarters with my friends and
contemplating the origin of mitochondria.
For Hyakutake, I was on the verge of getting
married. The only stars I remember were the ones
from lightheadedness. Each decade has had its
distractions that demanded I not spend nights
perfecting my gaze into the dark abyss.
I had to smooth the terrain where
my house of selves would be built.
I was responsible for following my plans.

Along the way I have missed opportunities
and waited for others that never came.
This is the creed of all skywatchers.
It requires patience for the center of the cosmos
to descend and freshen the power spots.
After that the listless seasons will be reanimated.
The tide will resume its stretching. The shape of
the moon will look like a shrine to the great deceiver
who tricks life into expecting order.
Once in a lifetime everything will be in alignment.
The possible seems ready. Once in a lifetime
there is a chance that offers only a wake of debris.

84

# Through the Nations of Mustard Fields

We escape from the Invented Garden, the spacious inland sea where the gargantuan plain teems with bunches of grass. The herds graze. The great flyway of birds attends to stolen glimpses of interstate, the silos stiffened and insistent on pointing at the ineffectual clouds. The landscape is patterned here and now with its holdings and enterprises, its phases of growth and incessant labor. There is always someone from somewhere coming to steady a hoe or drive a tractor across the hell of the valley's impressive acreage. There is someone who arrives and suddenly believes in every principle upheld by the tradition of escape.

    every crooked limb of riverine oak is tortured by its own growth;
    every half hidden stream mumbles its defiance, then submits
    and takes cover; every driver is forced to believe in the horizon.

We drive with a sympathy for the possibility in the wires hung overhead. The flies, the dust, the stink express their intimate service to place, to the mid-morning signs of crows contaminating the trees. They are the black flecks on this portrait of spring. The drizzle conditions a two-lane queue of drivers, one lone vehicle weaving in and out through the tangle. Always there is one too ready to meet the next somewhere, advancing into a permanent state of destination. The rain stimulates changes in how to view a landscape. The white egrets examine the wet scene patiently. They balance the crows with their innocence. They exist for our eyes to slowly follow their trace.

    a hundred data points along the highway and I have to pick one
    where a coyote has fallen. it comments on the roads that have been
    built, the long gray smile stretched and hinting at pleasure.

We start with the light on the vineyards and work towards accommodating a vision. The light rolls over the red Spanish tile roofs of the subdivisions. God bless the metastasis! The light moves like a whisper across an injured map. An expedition sets off for a legendary island exposed at the end of the Ice Age. Now and again it may be found by chance, but if one seeks it, it cannot be found. It is lost on the road to nowhere, appearing as a floating Eden raised by the red sails of evening beginning to emerge. We start with the light on the vineyards and end with dusk, a pleasure that runs from the Ice Age in the past to the Ice Age to come.

    the gaps in the storm clouds let light be thrown down. I catch it
    with the top of my brow, the shadow severe. my head perches and
    swivels like a dark thing ready to descend on Crows Landing.

We make a virtue of driving in the fast lane, take risks with our pros-
pects — we believe in order to see. The orchards let us inspect them,
but first we must insist there is plenty of fruit. Our hybrid car nurtures
a comfortable dream. Every seven years Hy-Brasil lists to starboard, and
the gatherers pad the coast to glimpse the ineffable mood of the sea.
They seek protection from its imagined venom, map the ocean floor to
find the hidden veins. We hold our hands out the window to catch the
particulates of the coming new religion.

    The loose fit of the green on the hills opposes the shimmer on
    the San Luis Reservoir feeding the aqueduct, the water's taut signature
    in an endless form of small waves. I gasp at its inability to play.

We hail the cleft in the hillside as the mover of earth shooting us the
moon. It is a friendlier gesture than a sober driver might imagine. We
take no offense at the attempt to burn its whims into our core. We
favor the role of current target, the chance to believe in the language it
has stored in its lumps and bruises, then released to our better nature.
Oh, ridiculous chimera of rock and animal by the roadside, ply us with
laughter as we count the lanterns of fishermen along the shore trying to
bring home something bigger.

    spotting individual artichokes in the fields, the heads of tiny natives.
    I understand each rut made by a truck as a sentence dedicated to
    the inner life of machinery, its slow viral crawl to the sea.

We climb the last hill in our sedan to view the blue origin of nowhere.
A wary sea awaits. We head into our escape downhill, thankful we have
happened upon driving as the new religion. Some say it is still just a
sport, but we are blessed, strapped in place within our moveable island.
We edge closer to the future without adhering to any established notion
of what ought to be. Today a little less land may belong to the sea,
tomorrow a little more. We make our stay at the threshold and unload,
our little pile of belongings enough to remind us of home.

    through the nations of mustard fields, through the tight and narrow
    turns of Pacheco Pass, the first blue wink of the bay from the shore,
    I see the gulls on the beach intimidating each other.

A gull steals the bag of trail mix and eats it on the treacherous rocks
where the tide pools hold the depth of the sky. I try to follow, but the
gull is smarter, outlasting me with the help of the wind. It glides to
the next sculpted ridge. My final destination is here among the hermit
crabs commuting back and forth in their basin, the shelf above full of
abalone, self-contained, like the ammonite thriving in the old salt spray.

# Wanderers

I took a vacation this year so I could get away
from my body. Before I left, I practiced getting
out of my body and leaving it sitting helpless
on a piece of furniture. I could disengage from
my heavy body faster than I could book a flight
to London on the internet. It came so easily; I left
for weeks. The papers piled up outside my
front door. But something went wrong and
now I can't get back in. Everywhere I wander
dead people are making fun of me.

They tell me I should eat more,
enjoy myself, let things fall where they may.
But I worry about the living, my body growing
slacker each day that I am gone.
I feel there might be gaps between heartbeats
where I could sneak back in. Maybe one of my
possessions would give me shelter while I
watched my limbs grow thin. There is only
time now to believe, and maybe only time
to show me how to become what I have left behind.

## The Alliance

Whose god is on my side?

The earth spins slower, the days are longer,
whose god is on my side?

The earth spins slower, the days are longer,
whose god is on my side?
I am repeatedly visited by neglect.

I am afraid to test the limits of the neuron.
The earth spins slower, the days are longer,
whose god is on my side?
I am repeatedly visited by neglect
but welcomed by a caravan of souls in the desert.

We convene at the moment of our making,
then spread out to distant outposts,
masquerading as independent creatures,

our hearts racing like a run on a gypsy cimbalom.
We would prefer to roam in a wilderness of mirrors.

My duty would be to face my faith in me.
Sh-h-h, I'm receiving a transmission now on how to be

a ladybug without spots,
        flying between an imaginary rose and a real one.

My caravan and I wander an unforgiven path,
tracing a cobbled form on the graph of our days together,

but I am afraid to test the limits of the neuron.
The earth spins slower, the days are longer,
whose god is on my side?

# The Call to Evening Prayer

I have begun to watch the shadows extend
themselves on the huge oaks outside my window
in the way that suggests dusk is soon to follow.
I realize that dusk marks more of an end than
a beginning and that this is somehow final, limiting.
The move toward light is seen as life-affirming.
But there are creatures stirring in the darkness too.
This moment of the failing day is the favorite
of the earth's most worthless creatures. There is
nothing more to do or say then. I resent that this moment
does not happen more often — it is the border between
the time for accomplishments and the time
for when those accomplishments are measured.
There are, however, some of us who work at night too.
We are the ones who refuse to bring any charge against
night's stillness as we calmly remember the pink
coming together with the orange in the evening sky,
when the lines of cars head for a small circle of ground
beyond the traffic.

# A Young Man's Salutation to the Night

Night, if I may, how should I address you this time or should
I just let my memory free itself of its obsession with you?
I should let your name take refuge in the realm beyond all
meaning. You could recover there with my misspent days,
the ones where I was sacrificed to my senses, unknowingly,
like a fool. I am just a young man, night,
but I know that you lie about your age.

Night, how you envelop the earth; you are this bright sphere's
edgeless beauty. Are you the wind blowing through forgotten
cities too? There is late talk among the candles that you are
the protector of these earthly virtues and evils, the ones
so complicated they can cover figures and desires entirely,
so no one can distinguish where the one begins and the other ends.
Then, in our good fortune, we wander in the daylight between
the statues of our making, noting how the sculptor resolved
the problem of the form. I am just a young man, night,
no stranger to idealism, but there is no reason to believe
I can choose my shape within the womb,
lying down within your dark warmth.

I am not afraid of you either. Nor can I determine what you are
considering when I lie awake within you. You are a vessel of
panic and suffering, aren't you? I give to you my useless hours,
the ones with which I cannot tame the age in which I'm living.
I was born among the scattershot stars, misaligned to reflect
our misgivings. And I could rage against this plan you seem
to be hatching for our mortal amusement, if I could call it
something. Night, you own a nameless agenda whose stealth
is legendary, a legend that does not bear repeating.
You press into my memory, but you mean nothing.
When I am in your presence, how shall I
address you — Mr., Mrs., Dr., Reverend, lover?
I only ask out of politeness, because your flat and lifeless
beauty allows me to give my whims their names.

# The Little Fool

A Cheerio, a ball of rice, a bit of scrambled egg
remain on the floor, and you are not there,
my confidant in the night, when I talk to your
grave with the little cypress growing on it.
Is this how Martin Luther spoke to God,
to clarify the errors of the spirit?
Is this the same night where he tooled
his famous scorn of princes? I relish
the flat tone of the night where I can
negotiate the world, its tumble into chaos
and reform, its heimliched virtues,
aware as I am that these negotiations
require massive bandwidth.

Tischgespräch: When one prays for another, the game
is in having someone listen, someone knock on
the door and ask for water, for directions, for
a light in the dark. Then one may continue,
granted that the mouth of death does not visit
in the private chamber and feed from one's
hand. The hand should be used to cover
the face in peek-a-boo fashion so that one may
become initiated into the order of fools.

I wake again before the paper comes
and whisper your name as if it were a guard
against intelligence. You came again to visit
last night and make your faces for my benefit.
The one that says: Chase me. The one that
says: Let's play. The one that says: You
gonna finish that? But the day starts with
another contest looming. A man in a foreign
land is claiming martial law to consolidate his
power, and I am a naked cloud with
seams, hanging over the demonstrations
in the city. I am there for the drama,
to see the imitation of power, to see whose
talent for apology will prevail. That was your
talent with your mouth wide open in the stupid
grin that said: let me lick the salt on your face.

Princes rule by force because the prevailing wickedness in the world
among the multitude is so great that without the prince's power to

suppress evil, the world would tumble into chaos.
        — Martin Luther

In France it is illegal name a pig Napoleon.
In California it is illegal to rob a bird's nest from a public cemetery.
In Massachusetts all dogs must have their hind legs tied down
        during the month of April.
In Miami it is illegal to publicly imitate animals.

Did I need to lick back, my friend?
My tongue was not as fast as yours.
I had no talent for the reciprocal kiss,
but you scrubbed the back of my hand
with your tongue, a courtier's gallant
gesture. You were there as we undressed,
ready to lap up the spillage like it was
afterbirth, the reason, I'm told, dogs began
to spend time around domesticated men.
I picked up your balls of fur on the rug.
I left the dishwasher door open.
You cocked your head when I whistled
the theme to Andy Griffith. We howled together,
call and response, at the steadily attendant moon.

Tischgespräch: When men see themselves abandoned by
all music in the night, they must be taught to sing,
for singing has nothing to do with the affairs of this
world. It is not the work of the gainsayers. It is not
for the law. If a man seeks good temperament for
all things the night bestows, for the headaches,
for the gross ignorance in the failings of books,
for the defects in original thinking, for the misconduct
of the mind, then let that man be skilled in singing.
We should not ordain young men to take care of
the night unless they have been well exercised in music.

*O death, O death, O death, where is thy sting?*
*O grave, where is thy victory?*

Be thou comforted, little dog, thou too in resurrection
shall have a little golden tail.
        — Martin Luther

There should be a law that every couple
thinking of getting married be required to

92

have sex while a dog is in the room.
This should be done with the idea in mind
that the dog is the surrogate child.
The test is to see how the heat of passion
affects a person's response to the needs
of the dog. If it barks and whines, should
all progress halt? Who will be the first
to stop and comfort it?

Tischgespräch: When a man studies under the auspices
of lawyers, he soon achieves perspective on the flawed
nature of existence so much as the word auspice means
"augury from the birds." From the heights he is allowed,
the man can play the part of master until he is forced
to submit to the acceptable juice of the cellar.
There he drinks as a heretic, a perverted creature, half-lame,
a monster, a fable, a nothing. There he drinks to prove
how much there is to gain.

In Oklahoma a person can be fined, arrested or jailed for making
            faces at a dog.
In Liverpool it is illegal for a woman to go topless unless she is a
            clerk at a tropical fish store.
In Utah birds have the right of way on all highways.
In Connecticut it is illegal to educate dogs.

Tonight is the first night of rain on your grave.
I keep talking to you about the man in the foreign land
with an abusive need to control the situation.
He places his opponent under house arrest.
I read to you from the Bible how the good kings
paid and maintained singers. I convince you
only that I am a fool with a head detonated
by too many streams of information.
If you were here, you'd educate me on
how the rain smells, the little hairs near
your nostrils quivering. The worms crawling
on the sidewalk. A hint of jasmine. The mud like
damp hair. The rotting jack-o-lantern caving in.
I feel stupid enough to let out a therapeutic howl:
            ow ow ow-w-w for something
            innocent entrusted to your care.

In his Table Talk, Martin Luther mentions his
puppy, Tölpel, who is at the table, looking for a

morsel and watching with open mouth and
motionless eyes. Martin Luther says, "Oh,
if I could only pray the way this dog watches
the meat! All his thoughts are concentrated
on the piece of meat. Otherwise, he has no
thought, or wish, or hope."

*I was walking through a dew-covered field, picking up speed as I hit the cross-wind,
when I heard Martin Luther calling out to me. He seemed to be interested in my
dog, Lucifer. He pointed out to me, "Look, how cheerfully he wags his tail though he
doesn't know where his next meal is coming from or whether men attending to their
power will be just in their delivery of it. Look, how he sniffs your boot and approves
of it, how he gazes at you through his eyebrows to challenge what you've been think-
ing. Look at how pure his trust is in everything around him." I corrected him, "this
dog is female, not male," but he went on talking about his dog who was somehow still
with him, still pressing his wet nostrils against his calf, still willing to scrape the cal-
luses of his hand with its tongue. He kept rubbing my dog between her ears and her
temples, and then in silence he moved off. As he walked away, I asked him, "What
is your dog's name?"*

       *"Tölpel," he said.*
       *"What does that mean"*
       *"It means 'little fool'"*

Tischgespräch: When heathen speak such fair and
excellent things of death, their heart is like quicksilver,
now here, now there, and so tomorrow. Therefore,
what the earth gives us today is seen as food and raiment
and is well-understood by the people. Though, too, a man
desires and longs after things that are uncertain.
Princes and kings seek it by raising great columns of stone.
The learned seek it with an everlasting book.
Only the honorable dog will fight lustily for it until
the other dogs are too strong for him and then,
as if a piece of meat, he will snatch a mouthful
lest he should lose it all.

Lots of people talk to animals.
Not that many listen though.
That's the problem.
       — Piglet

My friend writes a poem in which he and his wife
hold their convulsing dog right down to the end.
For them, it's a kind of prayer. It is not meant
to be answered. I listen in the dark for a signal

94

the night is becoming animal. The pigeons coo
on the roof across the street. A cat shrieks.
A cricket chirps in the doorway. In the distance
a dog barks maniacally the way you did
when you tried to bite the vacuum cleaner.
O, Lucifer, I come again to bemoan the fates
of men. Do you think if everyone had
a wagging tail to betray their thoughts,
this would make us more human?
Or would it be mandatory to cover it?
I open myself up to you who never knew
the full matter of what I was saying —
so foolish of me, so much better for it.
I am the wisest prince for letting you lick
my feet just out of the shower, for believing
your growl, for your tongue up my nose,
for your sniff at my sick days in bed,
for listening to your heart stop
little by little, watching your long pink tongue
fall out of your mouth. I speak up
to remind myself the night is empty
except for the meat of memory. I speak to
the unregulated murmur that builds up
to the last movement where the finale includes
a little cypress song, and at dawn I will listen
as the crazy neighbor's rooster crows.

**Tim Kahl** has been published in *Prairie Schooner, American Letters & Commentary, Berkeley Poetry Review, Caliban, Connecticut Review, Fourteen Hills, George Washington Review, Illuminations, Indiana Review, The Journal, Limestone, Nimrod, Ninth Letter, Notre Dame Review, Parthenon West Review, South Dakota Quarterly, The Spoon River Poetry Review, The Texas Review,* and many other journals in the U.S. He has translated German poet Rolf Haufs, Austrian avant-gardist, Friederike Mayröcker; Brazilian poets, Lêdo Ivo and Marly de Oliveira; and the poems of the Portuguese language's only Nobel Laureate, José Saramago. He also appears as Victor Schnickelfritz at the poetry and poetics blog *The Great American Pinup* (http://www.greatamericanpinup.blogspot.com) Additionally, he is also the editor for Bald Trickster Press (http://www.baldtricksterpress.com). He can also be found online at (http://www.timkahl.com).

LaVergne, TN USA
10 February 2010
172684LV00008B/5/P